PEANUTS® TREASURY

PEANUTS®
TREASURY

by CHARLES M. SCHULZ

Foreword by Johnny Hart

MetroBooks

2000 MetroBooks

ISBN 1-58663-068-7

Printed and bound in the United States of America

00 01 02 03 04 MC 9 8

RRD-C

For Meredith, Monte, Craig, Amy, and Jill

Foreword

A lot of years ago, a man named Oog sketched a bison on a cave wall, and a bunch of neighbors that saw it first hand were blabbing it about that Oog could knock out a bison that looked like the real item. Needless to say, Oog was the hit of every cookout for many years to follow.

Hosts would clink their leftover bones to get the attention of their guests and give Oog a tremendous introduction. Then Oog would whip out his red sable and a can of blackberry juice and knock out a fast bison on a nearby rock. The guests would poke one another in the ribs with their massive elbows and say: "How about that . . . just like the real item, eh?"

Oog got a little carried away with all this and began putting oversized humps on the bison and giving them big feet and funny noses. People noticed right off that this didn't look like the real item, so they started hissing and booing, a little mannerism they picked up from observing snakes and ghosts. Oog got the message, but was unperturbed with his critics. In his heart he knew he was reaching for a new art form that they did not yet comprehend, so the hisses and boos only added fuel to the fire of his fervor.

It will probably come as no surprise to those of you who are reading ahead, that Oog's illustrious career was dramatically foreshortened. Indeed, many among you who have seen someone trampled to death by a herd of angry, big-footed bison with funny humps, a species which had not yet learned to laugh at themselves, may be unimpressed to a fault.

It is hard to say why humans are able to laugh at themselves and bison are not. Since the very beginning, each era or generation has had its satirical cartoonist; one who stands above the others, points to what we have really become, and teaches us to laugh.

Our time has given us the best yet. He is Charles M. Schulz and it is an honor, not easily described, to be asked to write this Foreword for my friend and idol, particularly for a work of such importance as the undertaking of this book. Charlie Schulz and the "Peanuts" gang inspired, eleven years ago, my own decision to enter the comic strip world. Charlie is a dear man who has taken it upon himself to make children of us all. Let us be eternally grateful for his foresight. We are God's children after all, and are meant to be no more than that. As a jealous child who loves to laugh, I sometimes, with growing understanding, resent the laughs that God must surely enjoy at the expense of his clumsy, faltering children. He shares, of course, an equal amount of sorrow, which I do not wish to get into. Charlie Schulz does get into this. He gives us our pathetic side, and we laugh with dewy eyes.

One evening I read a strip which has Charlie Brown hesitating before the principal's office. He prays for the strength to face his ordeal, then like most of us who are not quite sure of that "mustard seed" bewails, "My stomach hurts." My wife and kids had to pry me off the floor with an abalone iron on that one. The "stomach" strip now hangs on a wall in my studio. There are times when Charlie Brown and the red-headed girl cause me more tears than laughter. Not knowing whether to cry or laugh is, at its best, an exhilarating feeling. We've all felt it. The invariable result is laughter, which feels good.

Charlie Schulz is a man who not only knows the intricate parts of the funny bone, but proves his knowledge day by day. All things to Schulz contain the element of fun. You and I and the world can rest assured that the day cannot come when a herd of angry, pumpkin-headed kids trample Charlie Schulz; he has already seen to that. They walk around three feet off the ground. Don't take my word for it, turn the page . . . see for yourself.

JOHNNY HART

Endicott, New York
August 1968

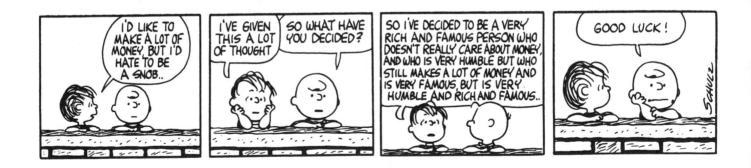

Panel row 1:

WHERE HAVE YOU BEEN? — CHURCH SCHOOL... WE'VE BEEN STUDYING THE LETTERS OF THE APOSTLE PAUL..

THAT SHOULD BE INTERESTING — IT IS..

ALTHOUGH I MUST ADMIT IT MAKES ME FEEL A LITTLE GUILTY...

I ALWAYS FEEL LIKE I'M READING SOMEONE ELSE'S MAIL!

Panel row 2:

DID YOU EVER STOP TO THINK THAT EVERY DAY IS SOMEBODY'S BIRTHDAY?

NO MATTER WHAT DAY IT IS, SOMEBODY IN THE WORLD HAS THAT DAY FOR A BIRTHDAY!

HAVE YOU EVER THOUGHT ABOUT THAT, CHARLIE BROWN? — NO, I CAN'T REALLY SAY THAT I HAVE...

YOU'RE GOING TO HAVE TROUBLE WHEN YOU GET TO COLLEGE!

Panel row 3:

EXERCISE, THAT'S WHAT WE NEED!

EVERYONE SHOULD START THE DAY WITH THIRTY PUSH-UPS!

HE'S RIGHT...

BUT HOW CAN YOU DO PUSH-UPS WHEN YOUR NOSE GETS IN THE WAY?

Panel row 4:

MY MOTHER HAS MADE ARRANGEMENTS FOR ME TO TAKE PIANO LESSONS...

I WON'T BE PLAYING ON A TOY PIANO EITHER... I'LL BE PLAYING ON A **REAL** PIANO!

YOU'RE CUTE WHEN YOU GET MAD...

Panel row 5:

HOW ARE YOUR PIANO LESSONS COMING ALONG?

FINE

YESTERDAY I LEARNED WHERE "MIDDLE C" IS...

CONGRATULATIONS

Row 4 (baseball strip):

Panel 1: MY HEART IS FULL ON THE DAY I FIRST GO OUT TO THE OL' BALL FIELD...

Panel 2: I LOVE THE SMELL OF THE HORSEHIDE, THE GRASSY OUTFIELD AND THE DUSTY INFIELD... I LOVE THE MEMORIES.. THE HOPES... AND THE DREAMS FOR THE NEW SEASON..

Panel 3: AH! THERE IT IS! MY PITCHER'S MOUND... COVERED WITH TRADITION..

Panel 4: AND DANDELIONS!

Panel 4: YOU'RE NOT HAPPY, ARE YOU?

Panel 1: CHARLIE BROWN, THERE'S A BOY OUTSIDE WHO PUSHED ME DOWN...

Panel 2: I TOLD HIM I'D GET MY BIG BROTHER AFTER HIM SO I WANT YOU TO GO OUT THERE, AND SLUG HIM

Panel 3: YOU MEAN YOU WANT ME TO GO OUTSIDE, AND FIND OUT WHAT HIS PURPOSE WAS IN PUSHING YOU DOWN, AND ASK HIM NOT TO DO IT AGAIN..

Panel 4: NO, I WANT YOU TO GO OUT THERE, AND **SLUG** HIM! / THAT'S WHAT I WAS AFRAID OF...

Panel 1: THAT BOY OUTSIDE PUSHED ME DOWN, AND YOU'RE AFRAID TO DO SOMETHING ABOUT IT! A FINE BROTHER YOU ARE!

Panel 2: ALL RIGHT! I'LL GO OUT THERE! I'LL EITHER TEACH HIM A LESSON, OR GET MYSELF KILLED!

Panel 3: THAT'S THE SPIRIT!! "SYDNEY OR THE BUSH"!

Panel 4: "SYDNEY OR THE BUSH"?

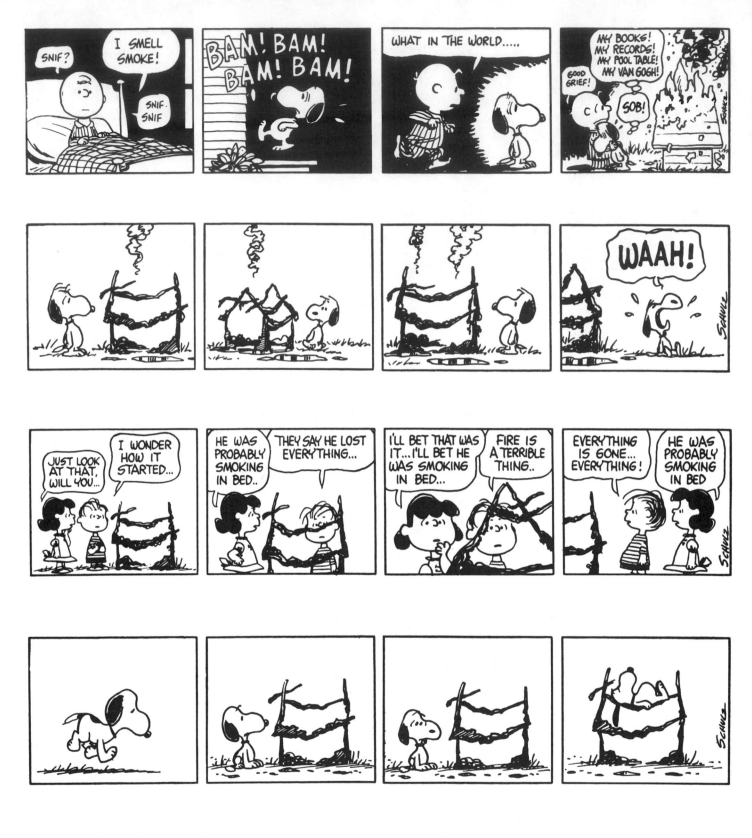